Metal Detecting Journal

The Best Way to Record, Log and Keep Track of Your Finds

Created by Mark Smith

D1570067

ISBN-13: 978-1506178882
ISBN-10: 150617888X
Metal Detecting Journal: The Best Way to Record, Log and Keep Track of Your Finds

Foreword

When I first started metal detecting I didn't keep track of any of my finds. I was all too eager to spend as much time as possible out there digging up more treasure. Who needed any kind of log book highlighting the past? I certainly did not.

I would separate the "real" treasure from all the trash at the first garbage can I could find. I was happy to rid my pockets of all the "trash" and get back out there digging up more treasure. It didn't take me very long to figure out this might not be the best idea.

Most of the supposed "trash" I was so eagerly depositing in the first garbage can that came around was still covered in dirt and grime from being buried under the soil for who knows how long.

One day it dawned on me that I might be tossing some very valuable items into the trash. Was I throwing away valuable history? Could I have tossed something of historical significance right into the old garbage can? You bet! That was the day I made the rule to never throw anything away without first cleaning and examining it.

I also had a really bad habit of taking all of the clad or junk coins I found and tossing them into an old five gallon bucket in my garage. One day my son saw me doing this and asked, "Why are you doing that dad?"

"They are all clad coins. They are only worth their current face value. I'll go through them later," I responded.

Later never did come. In fact, I filled one bucket pretty quick and over the course of a year of steady metal detecting, I managed to fill several buckets with nothing more than clad.

Going through these buckets of money didn't seem like all that much fun. So once again I convinced myself that I would take care of the money buckets later.

My son couldn't stand the idea of letting that much money sit in plastic buckets. He asked if he could go through one of them and I responded, "Sure, knock yourself out!"

He eagerly emptied the entire bucket right onto the floor of the garage. There must have been $500 or so in change laying in one heaping pile. Okay maybe it was only $100 or so. I can't really remember. I do know there were lots of coins, a lot more than I remember digging up.

My son was happily going through the huge pile of coins when he pulled out a silver Roosevelt dime. How did that get in there I wondered to myself. He found 4 more pieces of silver in the same bucket. After going through the first bucket, my son wanted to go through the rest of them. "Go for it!" I told him.

The same thing happened. He started finding a decent amount of coins that I had somehow overlooked. It could have my eagerness to get back out there or my aging eyes not being able to see the fine details in those dirty coins, but either way I was throwing some really good coins into these buckets.

My son said to me, "Dad, maybe you should keep track of all the stuff you find, ya know? Maybe you should have like a diary or a logbook where you write down all the cool stuff you find. That way you won't have this problem happen again."

What a great idea I thought. Why didn't I think of it?

While keeping track of all the great stuff you find with your metal detector may not be 100% necessary, but it can wind up being very beneficial.

Not only was I no longer tossing good valuable coins into buckets in the garage, I started to notice some patterns emerge in some areas I was regularly hunting. This led me to dig a little deeper so to speak and find even more treasures from the same spots.

I started recording my metal detector settings along with all of my finds and I started to notice that some settings seemed to outperform others. My metal detecting log books were turning out to be very helpful! Now instead of having buckets full of change in my garage. I had books that were loaded with very valuable information.

As time went by, I managed to fill quite a few notebooks. That was when I decided to make my very own metal detecting logbook. It was perfect for my needs and that is exactly what I am offering you in this book, a way to record and keep track of everything you find with your metal detector.

If you are not currently keeping track of all your finds, I highly encourage you to start by using this book. Who knows what kind of information you may uncover once you start keeping track all of your finds.

Entry #1

Date of find:	
Location or GPS coordinates:	

Items found:	

Value of finds:	

Machine used:	

Machine settings used:	

Notes or Comments:	

Entry #2

Date of find:	
Location or GPS coordinates:	

Items found:	

Value of finds:	

Machine used:	

Machine settings used:	

Notes or Comments:	

Entry #3

Date of find:	
Location or GPS coordinates:	

Items found:	

Value of finds:	

Machine used:	

Machine settings used:	

Notes or Comments:	

Entry #4

Date of find:	
Location or GPS coordinates:	

Items found:	

Value of finds:	

Machine used:	

Machine settings used:	

Notes or Comments:	

Entry #5

Date of find:	
Location or GPS coordinates:	

Items found:	

Value of finds:	

Machine used:	

Machine settings used:	

Notes or Comments:	

Entry #6

Date of find:	
Location or GPS coordinates:	

Items found:	

Value of finds:	

Machine used:	

Machine settings used:	

Notes or Comments:	

Entry #7

Date of find:	
Location or GPS coordinates:	

Items found:	

Value of finds:	

Machine used:	

Machine settings used:	

Notes or Comments:	

Entry #8

Date of find:	
Location or GPS coordinates:	

Items found:	

Value of finds:	

Machine used:	

Machine settings used:	

Notes or Comments:	

Entry #9

Date of find:	
Location or GPS coordinates:	

Items found:	

Value of finds:	

Machine used:	

Machine settings used:	

Notes or Comments:	

Entry #10

Date of find:	
Location or GPS coordinates:	

Items found:	

Value of finds:	

Machine used:	

Machine settings used:	

Notes or Comments:	

Entry #11

Date of find:	
Location or GPS coordinates:	

Items found:	

Value of finds:	

Machine used:	

Machine settings used:	

Notes or Comments:	

Entry #12

Date of find:	
Location or GPS coordinates:	

Items found:	

Value of finds:	

Machine used:	

Machine settings used:	

Notes or Comments:	

Entry #13

Date of find:	
Location or GPS coordinates:	

Items found:	

Value of finds:	

Machine used:	

Machine settings used:	

Notes or Comments:	

Entry #14

Date of find:	
Location or GPS coordinates:	

Items found:	

Value of finds:	

Machine used:	

Machine settings used:	

Notes or Comments:	

Entry #15

Date of find:	
Location or GPS coordinates:	

Items found:	

Value of finds:	

Machine used:	

Machine settings used:	

Notes or Comments:	

Entry #16

Date of find:	
Location or GPS coordinates:	

Items found:	

Value of finds:	

Machine used:	

Machine settings used:	

Notes or Comments:	

Entry #17

Date of find:	
Location or GPS coordinates:	

Items found:	

Value of finds:	

Machine used:	

Machine settings used:	

Notes or Comments:	

Entry #18

Date of find:	
Location or GPS coordinates:	

Items found:	

Value of finds:	

Machine used:	

Machine settings used:	

Notes or Comments:	

Entry #19

Date of find:	
Location or GPS coordinates:	

Items found:	

Value of finds:	

Machine used:	

Machine settings used:	

Notes or Comments:	

Entry #20

Date of find:	
Location or GPS coordinates:	

Items found:	

Value of finds:	

Machine used:	

Machine settings used:	

Notes or Comments:	

Entry #21

Date of find:	
Location or GPS coordinates:	

Items found:	

Value of finds:	

Machine used:	

Machine settings used:	

Notes or Comments:	

Entry #22

Date of find:	
Location or GPS coordinates:	

Items found:	

Value of finds:	

Machine used:	

Machine settings used:	

Notes or Comments:	

Entry #23

Date of find:	
Location or GPS coordinates:	

Items found:	

Value of finds:	

Machine used:	

Machine settings used:	

Notes or Comments:	

Entry #24

Date of find:	
Location or GPS coordinates:	

Items found:	

Value of finds:	

Machine used:	

Machine settings used:	

Notes or Comments:	

Entry #25

Date of find:	
Location or GPS coordinates:	

Items found:	

Value of finds:	

Machine used:	

Machine settings used:	

Notes or Comments:	

Entry #26

Date of find:	
Location or GPS coordinates:	

Items found:	

Value of finds:	

Machine used:	

Machine settings used:	

Notes or Comments:	

Entry #27

Date of find:	
Location or GPS coordinates:	

Items found:	

Value of finds:	

Machine used:	

Machine settings used:	

Notes or Comments:	

Entry #28

Date of find:	
Location or GPS coordinates:	

Items found:	

Value of finds:	

Machine used:	

Machine settings used:	

Notes or Comments:	

Entry #29

Date of find:	
Location or GPS coordinates:	

Items found:	

Value of finds:	

Machine used:	

Machine settings used:	

Notes or
Comments:

Entry #30

Date of find:	
Location or GPS coordinates:	

Items found:	

Value of finds:	

Machine used:	

Machine settings used:	

Notes or Comments:	

Entry #31

Date of find:	
Location or GPS coordinates:	

Items found:	

Value of finds:	

Machine used:	

Machine settings used:	

Notes or Comments:	

Entry #32

Date of find:	
Location or GPS coordinates:	

Items found:	

Value of finds:	

Machine used:	

Machine settings used:	

Notes or Comments:	

Entry #33

Date of find:	
Location or GPS coordinates:	

Items found:	

Value of finds:	

Machine used:	

Machine settings used:	

Notes or Comments:	

Entry #34

Date of find:	
Location or GPS coordinates:	

Items found:	

Value of finds:	

Machine used:	

Machine settings used:	

Notes or
Comments:

Entry #35

Date of find:	
Location or GPS coordinates:	

Items found:	

Value of finds:	

Machine used:	

Machine settings used:	

Notes or Comments:	

Entry #36

Date of find:	
Location or GPS coordinates:	

Items found:	

Value of finds:	

Machine used:	

Machine settings used:	

Notes or
Comments:

Entry #37

Date of find:	
Location or GPS coordinates:	

Items found:	

Value of finds:	

Machine used:	

Machine settings used:	

Notes or Comments:	

Entry #38

Date of find:	
Location or GPS coordinates:	

Items found:	

Value of finds:	

Machine used:	

Machine settings used:	

Notes or Comments:	

Entry #39

Date of find:	
Location or GPS coordinates:	

Items found:	

Value of finds:	

Machine used:	

Machine settings used:	

Notes or Comments:	

Entry #40

Date of find:	
Location or GPS coordinates:	

Items found:	

Value of finds:	

Machine used:	

Machine settings used:	

Notes or Comments:	

Entry #41

Date of find:	
Location or GPS coordinates:	

Items found:	

Value of finds:	

Machine used:	

Machine settings used:	

Notes or Comments:	

Entry #42

Date of find:	
Location or GPS coordinates:	

Items found:	

Value of finds:	

Machine used:	

Machine settings used:	

Notes or Comments:	

Entry #43

Date of find:	
Location or GPS coordinates:	

Items found:	

Value of finds:	

Machine used:	

Machine settings used:	

Notes or Comments:	

Entry #44

Date of find:	
Location or GPS coordinates:	

Items found:	

Value of finds:	

Machine used:	

Machine settings used:	

Notes or Comments:	

Entry #45

Date of find:	
Location or GPS coordinates:	

Items found:	

Value of finds:	

Machine used:	

Machine settings used:	

Notes or Comments:	

Entry #46

Date of find:	
Location or GPS coordinates:	

Items found:	

Value of finds:	

Machine used:	

Machine settings used:	

Notes or Comments:	

Entry #47

Date of find:	
Location or GPS coordinates:	

Items found:	

Value of finds:	

Machine used:	

Machine settings used:	

Notes or Comments:	

Entry #48

Date of find:	
Location or GPS coordinates:	

Items found:	

Value of finds:	

Machine used:	

Machine settings used:	

Notes or Comments:	

Entry #49

Date of find:	
Location or GPS coordinates:	

Items found:	

Value of finds:	

Machine used:	

Machine settings used:	

Notes or Comments:	

Entry #50

Date of find:	
Location or GPS coordinates:	

Items found:	

Value of finds:	

Machine used:	

Machine settings used:	

Notes or Comments:	

Entry #51

Date of find:	
Location or GPS coordinates:	

Items found:	

Value of finds:	

Machine used:	

Machine settings used:	

Notes or Comments:	

Entry #52

Date of find:	
Location or GPS coordinates:	

Items found:	

Value of finds:	

Machine used:	

Machine settings used:	

Notes or Comments:	

Entry #53

Date of find:	
Location or GPS coordinates:	

Items found:	

Value of finds:	

Machine used:	

Machine settings used:	

Notes or Comments:	

Entry #54

Date of find:	
Location or GPS coordinates:	

Items found:	

Value of finds:	

Machine used:	

Machine settings used:	

Notes or Comments:	

Entry #55

Date of find:	
Location or GPS coordinates:	

Items found:	

Value of finds:	

Machine used:	

Machine settings used:	

Notes or Comments:	

Entry #56

Date of find:	
Location or GPS coordinates:	

Items found:	

Value of finds:	

Machine used:	

Machine settings used:	

Notes or Comments:	

Entry #57

Date of find:	
Location or GPS coordinates:	

Items found:	

Value of finds:	

Machine used:	

Machine settings used:	

Notes or Comments:	

Entry #58

Date of find:	
Location or GPS coordinates:	

Items found:	

Value of finds:	

Machine used:	

Machine settings used:	

Notes or Comments:	

Entry #59

Date of find:	
Location or GPS coordinates:	

Items found:	

Value of finds:	

Machine used:	

Machine settings used:	

Notes or Comments:	

Entry #60

Date of find:	
Location or GPS coordinates:	

Items found:	

Value of finds:	

Machine used:	

Machine settings used:	

Notes or Comments:	

Entry #61

Date of find:	
Location or GPS coordinates:	

Items found:	

Value of finds:	

Machine used:	

Machine settings used:	

Notes or Comments:	

Entry #62

Date of find:	
Location or GPS coordinates:	

Items found:	

Value of finds:	

Machine used:	

Machine settings used:	

Notes or Comments:	

Entry #63

Date of find:	
Location or GPS coordinates:	

Items found:	

Value of finds:	

Machine used:	

Machine settings used:	

Notes or
Comments:

Entry #64

Date of find:	
Location or GPS coordinates:	

Items found:	

Value of finds:	

Machine used:	

Machine settings used:	

Notes or Comments:	

Entry #65

Date of find:	
Location or GPS coordinates:	

Items found:	

Value of finds:	

Machine used:	

Machine settings used:	

Notes or Comments:	

Entry #66

Date of find:	
Location or GPS coordinates:	

Items found:	

Value of finds:	

Machine used:	

Machine settings used:	

Notes or Comments:	

Entry #67

Date of find:	
Location or GPS coordinates:	

Items found:	

Value of finds:	

Machine used:	

Machine settings used:	

Notes or Comments:	

Entry #68

Date of find:	
Location or GPS coordinates:	

Items found:	

Value of finds:	

Machine used:	

Machine settings used:	

Notes or Comments:	

Entry #69

Date of find:	
Location or GPS coordinates:	

Items found:	

Value of finds:	

Machine used:	

Machine settings used:	

Notes or Comments:	

Entry #70

Date of find:	
Location or GPS coordinates:	

Items found:	

Value of finds:	

Machine used:	

Machine settings used:	

Notes or Comments:	

Entry #71

Date of find:	
Location or GPS coordinates:	

Items found:	

Value of finds:	

Machine used:	

Machine settings used:	

Notes or Comments:	

Entry #72

Date of find:	
Location or GPS coordinates:	

Items found:	

Value of finds:	

Machine used:	

Machine settings used:	

Notes or Comments:	

Entry #73

Date of find:	
Location or GPS coordinates:	

Items found:	

Value of finds:	

Machine used:	

Machine settings used:	

Notes or Comments:	

Entry #74

Date of find:	
Location or GPS coordinates:	

Items found:	

Value of finds:	

Machine used:	

Machine settings used:	

Notes or Comments:	

Entry #75

Date of find:	
Location or GPS coordinates:	

Items found:	

Value of finds:	

Machine used:	

Machine settings used:	

Notes or Comments:	

Entry #76

Date of find:	
Location or GPS coordinates:	

Items found:	

Value of finds:	

Machine used:	

Machine settings used:	

Notes or Comments:	

Entry #77

Date of find:	
Location or GPS coordinates:	

Items found:	

Value of finds:	

Machine used:	

Machine settings used:	

Notes or Comments:	

Entry #78

Date of find:	
Location or GPS coordinates:	

Items found:	

Value of finds:	

Machine used:	

Machine settings used:	

Notes or Comments:	

Entry #79

Date of find:	
Location or GPS coordinates:	

Items found:	

Value of finds:	

Machine used:	

Machine settings used:	

Notes or Comments:	

Entry #80

Date of find:	
Location or GPS coordinates:	

Items found:	

Value of finds:	

Machine used:	

Machine settings used:	

Notes or Comments:	

Entry #81

Date of find:	
Location or GPS coordinates:	

Items found:	

Value of finds:	

Machine used:	

Machine settings used:	

Notes or Comments:	

Entry #82

Date of find:	
Location or GPS coordinates:	

Items found:	

Value of finds:	

Machine used:	

Machine settings used:	

Notes or Comments:	

Entry #83

Date of find:	
Location or GPS coordinates:	

Items found:	

Value of finds:	

Machine used:	

Machine settings used:	

Notes or Comments:	

Entry #84

Date of find:	
Location or GPS coordinates:	

Items found:	

Value of finds:	

Machine used:	

Machine settings used:	

Notes or Comments:	

Entry #85

Date of find:	
Location or GPS coordinates:	

Items found:	

Value of finds:	

Machine used:	

Machine settings used:	

Notes or Comments:	

Entry #86

Date of find:	
Location or GPS coordinates:	

Items found:	

Value of finds:	

Machine used:	

Machine settings used:	

Notes or Comments:	

Entry #87

Date of find:	
Location or GPS coordinates:	

Items found:	

Value of finds:	

Machine used:	

Machine settings used:	

Notes or Comments:	

Entry #88

Date of find:	
Location or GPS coordinates:	

Items found:	

Value of finds:	

Machine used:	

Machine settings used:	

Notes or
Comments:

Entry #89

Date of find:	
Location or GPS coordinates:	

Items found:	

Value of finds:	

Machine used:	

Machine settings used:	

Notes or Comments:	

Entry #90

Date of find:	
Location or GPS coordinates:	

Items found:	

Value of finds:	

Machine used:	

Machine settings used:	

Notes or Comments:	

Entry #91

Date of find:	
Location or GPS coordinates:	

Items found:	

Value of finds:	

Machine used:	

Machine settings used:	

Notes or Comments:	

Entry #92

Date of find:	
Location or GPS coordinates:	

Items found:	

Value of finds:	

Machine used:	

Machine settings used:	

Notes or Comments:	

Entry #93

Date of find:	
Location or GPS coordinates:	

Items found:	

Value of finds:	

Machine used:	

Machine settings used:	

Notes or Comments:	

Entry #94

Date of find:	
Location or GPS coordinates:	

Items found:	

Value of finds:	

Machine used:	

Machine settings used:	

Notes or Comments:	

Entry #95

Date of find:	
Location or GPS coordinates:	

Items found:	

Value of finds:	

Machine used:	

Machine settings used:	

Notes or Comments:	

Entry #96

Date of find:	
Location or GPS coordinates:	

Items found:	

Value of finds:	

Machine used:	

Machine settings used:	

Notes or Comments:	

Entry #97

Date of find:	
Location or GPS coordinates:	

Items found:	

Value of finds:	

Machine used:	

Machine settings used:	

Notes or Comments:	

Entry #98

Date of find:	
Location or GPS coordinates:	

Items found:	

Value of finds:	

Machine used:	

Machine settings used:	

Notes or Comments:	

Entry #99

Date of find:	
Location or GPS coordinates:	

Items found:	

Value of finds:	

Machine used:	

Machine settings used:	

Notes or
Comments:

Entry #100

Date of find:	
Location or GPS coordinates:	

Items found:	

Value of finds:	

Machine used:	

Machine settings used:	

Notes or Comments:	

Entry #101

Date of find:	
Location or GPS coordinates:	

Items found:	

Value of finds:	

Machine used:	

Machine settings used:	

Notes or Comments:	

Made in the USA
Charleston, SC
29 January 2015